A Yum Lunch

By Carmel Reilly

Zan has a big box.

Dex set up.

He got six mats, six cups and a jug.

Zan cut up the buns.

She got the hot dogs.

Mum, Dad and Pop get fed.

Lex, Dex and Zan
get fed, too.

Mum pops yam jam
on the buns.

CHECKING FOR MEANING

1. What did Dex do to set up? *(Literal)*

2. Who got the hot dogs and cut up the buns? *(Literal)*

3. How do you know the family enjoyed their lunch? *(Inferential)*

EXTENDING VOCABULARY

box	What are the sounds in the word *box*? If you take away the *b*, what other letter could you put at the start to make a new word?
fix	What does *fix* mean? Talk about what Pop might do to fix the dip that Lex spilt.
yam	What is a *yam*? What other name can we give this food? What are the three sounds in this word?

MOVING BEYOND THE TEXT

1. What vegetables do you think are yum?

2. How were the children in this story helpful?

3. What jobs do you do to help out at home? Why?

4. What are other types of jam you can eat?

SPEED SOUNDS

Xx	Yy	Zz		

Kk	Ll	Vv	Qq	Ww

Dd	Jj	Oo	Gg	Uu

Cc	Bb	Rr	Ee	Ff	Hh	Nn

Mm	Ss	Aa	Pp	Ii	Tt

PRACTICE WORDS

box

Yum

Dex

Zan

yam

six

Lex

yum

Yam

fix